I.

Titles in Harvestime's **Pressure Points** series:

Hands Off!, by Roger Day
Hard Sell, by Roger Day
Dead Cert, by Roger Day
All Change, by Roger Day
Don't Call Me Chicken, by Peggy Burns
Far Side of the Shadow, by Peggy Burns
Henrietta Pudding, by Peggy Burns
The Web, by Peggy Burns
Breaking Out, by Liz Priestley
Hit and Run, by Liz Priestley
Second Best, bu Eunice Davies
Bed and Not Much Breakfast, by Christine Harris

Also by Roger Day:

Growing Up as a Christian (Word/New Frontiers)

With Christine Day:

Help! I'm Growing Up – A child/parent guide to sex and puberty
(Harvestime)

Hands Off!

Roger Day

Illustrations: Liz Priestley

Harvestime

Published in the United Kingdom by:
Harvestime Publishing Ltd, 69 Main Street, Markfield
Leicester LE6 0UT

First published by Harvestime
First printed March 1987
Reprinted July 1991

ISBN 0-947714-22-7

Typeset in the United Kingdom by:
ScribeTech Ltd, Bradford BD8 7BX
Printed and bound in the United Kingdom by:
Richard Clay Ltd, Bungay, Suffolk

Preface

'Get out, you pig. I hate you! I hate you!'

That's how Damien responded after his Uncle Bill came into the unlocked bathroom and abused him sexually.

The experience changed Damien from a happy, carefree boy into one full of hatred and bitterness. Even when he heard that his uncle was in prison, he wasn't satisfied. Now he wanted to see Uncle Bill killed.

That's when a man from his mum's church suggested that he, Damien, was also a prisoner — of his own hate, anger, bitterness and regret.

A book to help all boys and girls who have been sexually abused themselves or whose friends have gone through similar traumatic experiences.

To

all children who have been sexually abused

Contents

1

What a birthday!

I slammed my knife and fork on the plate, scattering sausages and chips on the table.

'Tell him, Mum,' I shouted, pointing at my kid brother Daniel, who was sitting opposite me beside his twin sister, Donna.

'Look, you two. If you don't stop arguing . . . .'

'It wasn't me. It was Damien,' sneered my brat brother.

He's the kind of kid that gets you. He's only eight but he's got a mouth like a coalhole with a voice like a foghorn to go with it. Donna's the opposite. She's quiet, kind and wouldn't hurt a fly.

The argument started over something very silly.

Dad was telling one of his awful jokes. 'Which is right?' he asked me. 'The yoke of an egg *is* white or the yoke of an egg *are* white?'

Like a fool, I fell for it hook, line and sinker. 'The yoke of an egg *is* white, of course,' I told him, feeling proud of my English ability.

'Wrong!' he replied with a cheesy grin. 'The yoke of an egg are *yellow!*'

Everyone roared with laughter, even Mum and Donna, who hardly ever laugh out loud unless they think something's extremely funny.

My kid brother carried on laughing and making fun of me. So I gave him a bit of a tap under the table with my foot. He howled as if he was dying.

The next second he was kicking me for all he was worth using both feet. I reckoned I'd have the bruises on the front of my legs for weeks. That's when I stopped eating and slammed down my knife and fork.

'Trust *him* to spoil my birthday, the pig. I wish he was dead!' I spat the words out, meaning every one of them.

Dad looked at me so hard it was like being stabbed with daggers.

'You know something, Damien,' he said, letting his knife and fork clatter on the plate. 'You haven't been the same boy since your last birthday.'

Boy, that hurt. The trouble was, he was right. Just the littlest thing made me lose my temper. I'd have fights, even with my best friends. I often lay awake for ages trying to get to sleep. And when I *did* sleep I'd have horrible nightmares that just wouldn't go away — even in the morning.

Dad didn't know, but that last birthday was a turning point in my life. Instead of having just a kid's party, my treat for the day had been a trip to the cinema to see a brand new space adventure film.

Somehow, Uncle Bill — the scrounger in our family, Mum calls him — managed to talk my dad into taking him along as well. So I ended up sandwiched between my least favourite uncle and the worst brother in the world.

Uncle Bill was one of those people you loved and hated both at once. He was great at computer games — especially *Aliens in Space* — and could tell some really funny stories. But he never knew when you'd had enough. He'd sometimes follow me to my bedroom and talk for what seemed like hours and hours when I just wanted a bit of peace and quiet.

He did the same sort of thing in the twins' bedroom. Sometimes I heard them complaining about it.

He was always scruffy and had smelly breath. I think it was because he lived on his own and smoked cigarettes all the time.

Anyway, there I was sitting watching this great film and trying to hear above the racket my kid brother was making.

Suddenly, I felt a hand on my knee. It was Uncle Bill's. He'd leaned across to say something to my dad and made it seem as if it was an accident that his hand had landed there.

Half an hour later it had moved up my leg and was now resting in a place where it shouldn't have been. The film was nearly over and had reached the most exciting bit, but I couldn't concentrate.

The strange thing was, I knew it wasn't an accident but I pretended to myself that it was. I think Uncle Bill pretended, too, because he didn't move his hand anymore and took it away quickly when the lights came on.

That, I reckoned, was the day my life started changing for the worse.

* * *

'Where are you now, son?' It was my dad speaking.

I shook my head to wake myself out of the daydream I was in. 'Oh, I don't know. I just don't feel very well.'

I shoved my chair back from the table, making an ear-piercing scraping noise on the tiled floor that made Donna jump a mile. Then I began walking heavily upstairs to my room.

Mum shouted out after me: 'I expect you'll feel better in a minute. I'll bring you some of your favourite pudding — just in case.'

Trust Mum. She seemed to understand, even if she didn't know what the trouble was. I'd thought of telling her or Dad about Uncle Bill, but I just couldn't get the courage. Anyway, I was sure no one would believe me.

'I hope that rat of an uncle of mine gets shot down by aliens from space,' I snarled as I flung myself on the bed.

Five minutes later, even though it was only seven o'clock in the evening, I fell into a restless sleep.

2

Enemy attack

I was in this incredible dream. There were alien spaceships flying round everywhere. I was hiding in a kind of bunker in dark woods, trying to eat my rations — yes, you've guessed it, cold sausages and chips!

Suddenly, I tossed my rations to one side as a whole battalion of spaceships began weaving their way through the trees of the forest.

I held my laser rifle to my shoulder, watching the leading spaceship through the image-intensified sights. I could see clearly the booster rockets and the strange, eerie flashing lights around the ship's sides.

With my other hand I adjusted the magnification so that I could get a close-up of the ship's commander. There he was, head forward as he concentrated on his target — me!

A second later a cold shiver ran down my spine. 'No! It can't be true!' I said to myself in an instant. But there was no mistaking that man — the greasy, grey hair, staring eyes and two-day-old stubble on his chin. It was Uncle Bill!

My finger tightened on the trigger, ready to make a killing. I was shaking from head to foot with a combination of excitement and fear.

'Now!' I said out loud, squeezing the trigger.

I expected to see a huge fireball as the spaceship caught the ray and blew to smithereens. Instead, nothing! I squeezed again. Still nothing. The trigger was jammed!

I banged the laser rifle with my other hand, hoping against hope that it would free itself. But nothing happened.

All this time Uncle Bill in his enemy spacecraft was getting closer and closer. I saw a broad grin crease his evil face. Then he lifted one hand from the controls and reached out as if he were trying to touch me like he did in the cinema. The hand seemed to get larger and larger as he came nearer. Soon it was all I could see.

The hand was on my knee now. I could see the long, dirty fingernails as I felt the hand slowly begin to move its way up my leg.

I let out a scream. 'No!' I shouted. 'Go away, Uncle Bill.

'No! No! Nooooooooooo!'

* * *

My heart was racing and my face covered in sweat as I opened my eyes. For a few seconds I was still in the forest facing the enemy attack, feeling that hand touching me again. Then, slowly, I became aware of the familiar wallpaper and furniture of my bedroom. It was only another nightmare after all.

Wiping the sweat from my forehead, I looked down the bed and noticed that I was lying on top of the covers with my clothes still on. Then I remembered last night's disastrous birthday supper.

It was beginning to get quite light in my bedroom but somehow I knew it was still very early. A quick glance at my watch confirmed what I'd already guessed — it was just after five in the morning.

Quickly I went to the toilet, got undressed and slipped on my pyjamas. By now, most of the details of the dream had gone from my mind, at least temporarily. My hope was that I would forget the whole thing.

I lay back on the pillow, staring at the ceiling. The ceiling of my bedroom has small cracks in it as well as those funny bumps made with a kind of thick paint. I tried to make pictures out of the patterns to help me get to sleep. But every time I tried, I merely saw alien spaceships — and my nightmare flooded back into my mind.

With a bit of imagination, one of the patterns looked like Uncle Bill. I swallowed hard as I noticed it. Pouring into my mind now were the times he had come to our house — usually uninvited — and sat down with us to watch TV after Daniel and Donna were in bed. Somehow, even if I was on the other side of the room, he always managed to worm his way into sitting next to me.

His excuses wore a bit thin.

'Damien likes me sitting next to him.'

'I've got this eye trouble and need to be nearer the screen.'

'I'll move to the sofa. After all, I wouldn't want to spill coffee on your best armchair, would I?'

I didn't want to create a scene so I usually stayed put. Mum and Dad never seemed to realise what he was up to.

Inevitably, once he was next to me, Uncle Bill would put his arm around me or rest his hand on my leg. Either way, he managed to touch me where he shouldn't.

I didn't dare tell anyone about it. If Mum and Dad found out, I reckoned they'd probably blame *me*. The twins were too young to talk to about it. Anyway, Donna might get upset. And as for Daniel, he'd just make fun of me.

* * *

It seemed like years before morning came. I kept seeing Uncle Bill coming towards me with a horrible grin on his ugly face.

Then the regrets started. 'If only I'd had my laser rifle properly serviced before the battle.'

'I should have eaten those cold sausages and chips instead of dropping them to the forest floor.'

'Maybe if I'd been wearing my padded spacesuit he wouldn't have been able to touch me in that way.'

'It was my fault really. If only . . . . If only . . . . If only . . . .'

I was sure I'd been awake the whole time, but I must have drifted off because, when I opened my eyes, I had to blink several times because of the bright sunlight streaming through a gap in the curtains.

On my dressing table was a bowl of delicious-looking trifle that Mum must have left for me the previous night. I ate it like a man starving in the desert who had just found a morsel of food.

Slowly, ever so slowly, I got dressed. It was a new day but, as usual, the memory of Uncle Bill just wouldn't go away.

3

Murder in the bike shed

After a quick breakfast I went out to the garden shed ready to work on my bike. That machine was my pride and joy, the ultimate dream of any cycling enthusiast. It had an ultra-lightweight Reynolds 531 frame, 12-speed dérailleur gears, drop handlebars and slick (treadless) tyres for low rolling resistance.

Most kids my age have stunt bikes or ones with small wheels. Mine is a proper racer, ideal for riding miles and miles at top speeds. I didn't have much time for all this clowning around with fancy two-wheeled toys.

My birthday presents of the previous day were mainly things to go with my bike. Best of all I had a really brill cycle computer that gives speed, trip distance in miles and kilometers and total distance, as well as such things as average speed, fastest speed and cadence rate.

Another thing I'd been given was a wedge bag that fits under the saddle, used for carrying things without causing too much wind resistance. There were also a couple of reflectors and an aerodynamic water bottle complete with wire cage — so that you can drink while you're riding along.

I'd been hoping to get some new cycling clothes. The cycling top and shorts I had were secondhand and were threadbare in places. And I wore ordinary trainers on my feet. 'You'd grow out of expensive cycling shoes in no time,' Mum said apologetically yesterday after I'd opened all my presents.

I wanted to fit all the new things on my bike so that I could use them for the last day or two of my school summer holidays.

But first I decided to strip down the whole bike, check and clean all the parts, then put everything back together, hopefully in the right order! Dad, who has always been good at practical things, taught me how to do it all and watched me do it twice on my old bike. I was sure I could manage myself this time, even though the bike was so much more expensive.

Everything went well as I took off the chain and gear mechanism and then the wheels. Then I began stripping down the moving parts, cleaning them in paraffin, rinsing them in water, letting them dry and finally regreasing them before fitting them back together.

I had to stop for an early lunch (trust Mum!), but by two o'clock I was making good progress.

Then I noticed one or two little problems. Some of the steel balls in the wheel bearings seemed a bit pitted. So were the bearing cups in the bottom bracket. There was also a broken spoke. I thought of forgetting about it but Dad always says: 'If you're going to do a job, do it well.' I knew he was right.

Mum was happy to let me have the bus fare to the

bike shop. But she told me to use some of my birthday money to pay for the parts. I didn't mind really. After all, apart from football, cycling was my main hobby.

The long bus ride through the busy city centre traffic gave me time to think. During the trip I decided to go on a cycling tour the next day to take my mind off things, get a bit of exercise — and test out my bike.

My plan was to pack my new wedge bag with a picnic lunch and fill my bottle with orange juice. I'd clip my plastic map holder on the handlebars and follow the route past the reservoirs where I used to go fishing with Dad.

It was funny really. I used to enjoy going out with Dad, just the two of us. But for the last year or so, even though I still loved to go fishing, I'd preferred to be on my own. It's as if I'd gone off *people* somehow!

Mum's always telling me to watch out for strangers who might do nasty things to me. I'm very careful not to stop and talk to anyone I don't know, but I reckon they can't do much worse to me than Uncle Bill.

When I got back home I carefully put the rest of the bearings back together and adjusted the pedal mechanism. Fitting the new spoke was a bit of a pain. I had to take off the tyre and inner tube, slip off the rim tape and unscrew the old one before I could fit it in.

Then I adjusted the front and rear dérailleur, fixed on the new parts, cleaned the bike with soapy water and gave it a good shine with Mum's spray polish.

Once all that was done I took it for a test run.

There was just one last adjustment needed to the

gears. Back in the shed I bent to make the adjustment and stood up quickly, smashing my head on an old metal bedframe that Dad planned to take to the junkyard one day.

For a second all I saw were stars. It hurt so much that it took my breath away. Then, almost instinctively, I lashed out with my foot, kicking the bedframe angrily.

That made things even worse. Now my foot was hurting as well as my head! In fury I grabbed a rusty old crowbar that Dad had left lying around and began beating the frame with all my strength.

'Take that, you evil piece of scrap metal,' I yelled. The crowbar vibrated with the blow, sending shockwaves right up my arm to my shoulder. 'You're almost as nasty as Uncle Bill — if that's possible.'

'I'm going to kill you,' I shouted between clenched teeth, bringing the crowbar crashing down yet again.

'Die, Die, Die!' Each time I shouted I smashed the bedframe harder and harder. My arm was aching and I was gasping with exhaustion from the effort. But still I carried on and on and on.

Gradually, in between the ear-shattering vibrations of the blows, I sensed that someone else was in the shed. Turning round sharply I saw my little sister, Donna, standing staring at me. Her head was tilted slightly, eyes wide open and freckly face totally expressionless. Wisps of her blonde hair had fallen across her face and a few strands were in her mouth.

A flicker of fear crossed her brow. She opened her mouth as if to say something but changed her mind and snapped her mouth closed as if she were a shark capturing its prey.

For a moment I was too stunned to speak. Then I recovered enough to get my words out.

'Oh — er — hi!' I said with a forced smile. 'I'm just — er — having a smashing time.'

The joke went down like a lead balloon.

'Mum says its teatime.' She spoke without a trace of emotion.

'Oh good,' I replied. 'I've just finished anyway.'

I threw down the crowbar, locked the shed and held Donna's hand as we walked in silence towards the back door. I hoped and prayed that she hadn't heard what I'd said about Uncle Bill.

If she told Daniel, I knew that everyone in the world would find out within 10 minutes!

4

Lost freedom

It was good to feel the cool wind in my face as I cycled through the open countryside. I enjoyed the thrill of going downhill at high speeds and taking corners to the limits of my bike's road-holding ability.

This was my day out — and I was going to enjoy it to the full.

I looked at the fields of ripened wheat on both sides of the road. It was such a lovely sight.

Everywhere farmers were busy gathering in the crops. There were huge red combine harvesters chopping down the corn and sifting out the grain. And there were tractors pulling hay balers that picked up the loose straw and formed it into large brick-shaped bales. Dad always calls those bales 'giant's shredded wheat', though I can't imagine what they'd taste like with milk on!

Suddenly I saw coming towards me on the other side of the road a large blue tractor pulling a trailer loaded high with straw bales. As it approached I knew from the tractor's deep, roaring sound that it was one of the top-of-the-range Fords.

It passed, scattering loose strands of straw on me and over the road. On its side were the words: 'Ford 7600'. I'd been right. In our house we all like tractor spotting — even Mum — and have got quite expert at recognising the different makes and sizes. And when we spot a Zetor or some other less common tractor, Donna and Daniel get really excited.

It was a perfect day to be out on the road. There were only a couple of annoyances. Once or twice I had to cycle into the wind — uphill at the same time. I hate doing that. It slows you down so much you think you're going to stop.

The other thing that made me cross was having a puncture. I was glad I'd brought a spare inner tube. Using the tyre levers in my wedge bag I was soon back on the road. Later, I'd repair the puncture at home.

I was determined not to daydream while I was cycling. The only time I did that ended in disaster.

It was last October and I was out on my old bike. I'd been on a long cycling trip and was nearly back home. I was wearing a long-peaked cap that my grandad had brought back from a trip to Canada.

There I was thinking about the horrible events of the previous couple of weeks involving Uncle Bill. I'd drifted into a kind of daze and, without realising it, my head had got lower and lower so that I could only see the road immediately in front of me.

The next moment I'd been lying on the roof of the parked car I'd just crashed into! I felt a real idiot, though I wasn't hurt much. Everyone made fun of me when I told them the story. I joined in the laughter even though I was hurting inside.

The bike was a write-off. Wheel. Front fork. Frame. Just about everything on it was bent or broken. It would have cost too much to repair. I wondered if my cycling days were over.

That Christmas my parents and both sets of grandparents put their money together and bought me the best present I've ever had — my racing bike.

It wasn't a new one. Dad told me he'd seen the advert for this secondhand bike that a boy had grown out of. It turned out that his parents had more money than sense and had bought the most expensive bike in his size they could find. Even secondhand, though, the bike was far more than Mum and Dad could normally have afforded.

Now, with the extra fittings, I was enjoying my bike to the full.

After a lazy lunch I lay back on the grass in the warm midday sun, closed my eyes and began to relax.

Straightaway my mind began to fill with thoughts of the worst day in my life. It's always been something I've wanted to bury in the past. The trouble is, I can remember it as if it were yesterday.

That evening my Uncle Bill had shown up on the doorstep. If it had been left to me I would have told him to get lost but, typical of Mum, she invited him in.

'You might as well make yourself useful and babysit for us. Jim and I are going out tonight. I'll cancel the babysitter.'

'Aw Mum,' I groaned when he'd gone up to tuck Daniel and Donna in bed. 'Can't the babysitter come as well? She's nice and tells lots of great stories.' It wasn't true but I had to use some excuse to avoid being on my own with Uncle Bill yet again.

'No. Bill, um, Uncle Bill, is perfectly capable of taking care of you three, specially as the twins are already in bed. Anyway, he needs to do something for his living. He's always scrounging meals.'

I've learnt from years of experience that there's no point in arguing with my parents.

After a quick peck on the cheek from Mum as she and Dad dashed out of the door, I sat down and flicked on the telly. It was the usual boring stuff.

After a lot of noise upstairs, with Daniel shouting 'No, no' all the time, Uncle Bill came down and plonked himself in the armchair, trying to read this big newspaper. All the pages were flopping down around him like a tent with ten layers of canvas.

I knew what would happen if I sat watching the telly. He'd come over, sit beside me and then start inching up towards me. I wasn't having it this time.

'I'm going to have a bath,' I announced. Me, wanting to be clean! It seemed such a weak excuse.

'Oh. Right then. See you later.' He looked back at his paper as if he wasn't interested where I was just going.

I nipped upstairs, turned on the taps and threw my clothes in a big heap on the floor. It was good to lie back in the warm water, just enjoying a bit of peace without that noisy brother of mine.

The twins were asleep by now. I knew that because the house had gone silent.

I must have been in a bit of a daydream. Suddenly, the door began to open. I nearly jumped out of my skin. Then I saw who it was.

'Uncle Bill, do you mind? What are you doing in here?'

'Oh, it's alright, Damien. I was just feeling a bit lonely downstairs.'

I could have kicked myself for not locking the door.

He walked slowly over to the bath and knelt down beside it. Then I watched as those shifty grey eyes of his looked me up and down. Talk about being embarrassed!

'You're growing up fast, old boy.' I secretly hated the way he called me 'old boy' whenever he was trying to be extra friendly.

I followed his eyes down the front of my body. 'I . . . I . . . don't know what you mean,' I said hesitantly.

'Oh, I think you do, really,' he replied nervously, placing his hand on my soggy wet shoulder. 'You're becoming a proper young man and I think it's high time you learned a thing or two.'

I could see his body shaking. His voice sounded a bit like a strangled parrot. He didn't say anything as he moved his quivering hand slowly, ever so slowly, down my chest and over past my tummy.

My body started responding to the advancing hand even before it had reached its destination. I couldn't help it. The response was complete just a few seconds after he began touching me.

I suppose I should have shouted 'No!' like we'd been taught to do at school. But I was paralysed with fear.

It was a million times more horrible than I could ever imagine. For a start, he was rough, almost vicious. But much, much worse was the way I felt as if something was being taken away from me. I was being robbed — and the robber wouldn't stop his stealing.

I began to realise how a girl or woman must feel when she's being raped. The pain might go away but the horrible feelings in your mind linger on and on.

The worst thing about it was when he started kissing me, slobbering all over me as if I was his latest girlfriend. It was horrible. I wiped away the smelly spit from my mouth and cheek.

It's difficult to describe the way I felt when he'd finished. Somehow it seemed as if I was suddenly unclean, dirty inside. Guilt swept over me like the waves of the sea.

'That's nice. That's nice,' he hissed as he stopped. 'You're a real man now, you know, Damien,' he said, trying to force a relaxed smile.

Real man! If only I'd been man enough to shout and scream and lash out at him before it had gone this far. If only I'd never decided to have a bath in the first place this horrible thing wouldn't have happened to me.

Uncle Bill's desperate-sounding whisper of a voice snapped me back into reality. 'Now, how about doing the same for me?' he said.

I couldn't think of anything worse. Anger welled up within me. But instead of shouting my refusal, I did the one thing that came into my head. I spat at him!

It was the first time I'd done that to anyone — and the last! Despite the way I felt, I had to smile. It was a direct hit. The frothy saliva was now dribbling down his stubbly cheek.

That didn't stop him messing with himself, though. He was so desperate that it was all over in about ten seconds. Then, gasping for breath, he put his arm back round my shoulder.

'I'm sorry, old boy.' His body was still shaking but his voice was returning to normal. 'I didn't mean to upset you. I . . . just . . . couldn't help it.'

I glanced at my uncle. For a split second I almost felt sorry for this pathetic heap of human trash. Then the anger inside me exploded as I threw his hand off my shoulder.

'Get out, you pig. I hate you! I hate you!' I yelled. I knew I'd start thumping him if he hung around much longer. A moment later I heard the front door slam as he rushed away from our house.

Then I lay back in the bath and cried and cried just like my little brother.

It was the last time I ever saw my Uncle Bill.

5

A day with Daniel

It was funny how I felt when I first heard that Uncle Bill was in prison. There was relief and hate mixed with a twinge of guilt.

Mum mentioned it one day without saying why he'd been put inside. I didn't need to guess very hard. He'd probably done to other kids the same sort of thing he'd done to me — and one of them had grassed on him by telling the police.

I remembered back to the time he came into the unlocked bathroom, did his evil deed to me and then ran away like a frightened rabbit. When Mum and Dad got home that night I told them he'd just disappeared on me.

Mum said: 'Typical Bill,' and never mentioned it again.

Now they'd caught him and I was pleased. 'I hope he dies in prison,' I said under my breath, meaning every word. Yet deep inside I still had a feeling of guilt as if *I* were to blame for what happened and for him going to prison.

Gradually over the months that followed I let my

imagination run wild, dreaming up worse and worse tortures to make his life in prison more miserable. I started remembering pictures in my history book of old-fashioned kinds of torture.

'Wouldn't it be ace if Uncle Bill was put in the stocks and I could pelt him with rotten eggs and mouldy rubbish?'

'How about torturing him with a thumbscrew, tearing his hand apart with the last twist?'

'Stick him on the rack and stretch his arms and legs until they pull out of their sockets.'

A mock smile creased my face as I planned these tortures. I knew some people called it spite but I hated every memory of that horrible, horrible pig of a man.

* * *

'Which way, Damien? Which way?

'Damien? Damien? *Damien?*'

I shook my head to wake myself out of the daydream I was in. My little brother Daniel was standing beside me saying the same thing over and over again like a record that's stuck. And I wasn't even listening.

'Oh, er, I don't know yet,' I replied, looking at the Ordnance Survey map in my hand. 'Yes, it's that path,' I said, pointing to the right.

It was nice being out in the countryside, enjoying the peace and beauty. But it seemed strange having to spend the last free day of the summer holidays with my rotten kid brother.

I suppose it was my fault, really. Right at the beginning of the holidays, in one of my weaker moments, I'd promised to take Daniel out walking for the day. And especially since Mum started going to church and calling herself a Christian, she's insisted that I keep my promises.

Our house is in a council estate right on the edge of the city. From a distance you can see the estate perched on the hillside in the middle of farmland as if it had been dropped there from outer space.

Most kids who live on the estate hate it because they haven't got much to do except break down fences and vandalise the farmland. I love it because you can watch the farmers at work, go for walks and bike rides in the country and just get away from it all.

That day we started our walk and were in the countryside in less than a minute! That's what I call a nice place to live.

I looked down at my little brother walking beside me. He's a bit of a shrimp for his age and he's skinny to go with it. I sometimes think he'd make a good subject for an Oxfam poster.

He's got blue eyes and blond hair and can put on a cheeky smile. Lots of grown-ups go all gooey about this sweet, innocent little boy. I know the truth. At home he's a real pain, always wanting to do what I'm doing, getting me into trouble and generally making a nuisance of himself.

I guess he's alright really, but since Uncle Bill started making his approaches to me, I haven't been very patient and I'm no good at controlling my temper.

Looking at him reminded me of the last time the two of us had been out walking together. It was just a few weeks after the incident in the bath.

As we were walking along, I suddenly decided to do to Daniel what Uncle Bill had done to me. I don't know why, really.

Daniel seemed bored with what I was doing to him. After about 30 seconds, though, I started to get rough with him. I was thinking of Uncle Bill at the time. For some awful reason I wanted to hurt Daniel like my uncle had hurt me.

'Ouch,' he shouted. 'Don't do that, Damien. I don't like it.'

Suddenly he seemed to remember what he'd been taught at school. 'No!' he said firmly, glaring at me. 'No, no, no!'

He was making so much racket that I panicked and stopped. Then he dashed off to climb a tree as if nothing had happened.

He never mentioned it again, so it probably didn't have much effect on him. But it made me feel as if I was some evil monster.

Now I started blaming myself for not complaining like Daniel did to me when Uncle Bill first touched me. I felt guilty that I hadn't screamed at my uncle when he first came into the bathroom. I considered it my fault that he had gone to prison — and I wondered if I should go there, too, because of what I'd started doing to Daniel.

Anyway, this day in the countryside had been almost enjoyable so far. We'd walked all morning, played in the woods for a while after lunch and then started for home. We'd had a lot of stops on the way, looking at squirrels scuttling about in the trees, farmers working in their fields and even a couple of rabbits hopping across the path.

I began to wonder if, deep inside me, I'd agreed to go on this walk as a way of making up to Daniel for what I'd tried to do to him. We'd only had two arguments all day and now we were just half a mile from home.

That's when trouble struck. We'd come to this fork in the path. According to the map, the path to the right was the way home. Daniel got it into his head that we should go on the one to the left. I think he was just feeling tired and awkward.

'Look,' I said, pointing to the map. 'The path to the right leads home.'

'No it doesn't,' he whined. 'I know you're wrong. You're just trying to get us both lost!'

'Don't be such a baby,' I said sharply. 'Just follow me.'

'No, I won't,' he replied, stamping his foot.

'You silly little kid,' I replied through clenched teeth.

That's when he started thumping me as if I was a boxer's punchbag. I finally lost my cool.

'Right, you go that way and I'll go the proper way. And then we'll see who's right!'

Without a word he stomped off down his path and I continued the walk home.

* * *

Half an hour after I'd sat down next to my sister, Donna, to watch TV, Mum called from the kitchen.

'Damien, where's Daniel?'

'Uh? Oh, I dunno.'

A few minutes later she walked in with a half-opened packet of sliced bread in her hand. 'Dad'll be home for his supper in a minute. Have you seen Daniel anywhere since your walk? He *did* come back with you, didn't he?'

I hung my head a bit, feeling a twinge of regret. 'No, he went on a path of his own so I left him to it.'

'You *what?'* The bread made a dull thud as Mum dropped it to the floor.

'Well, it wasn't my fault,' I pleaded. 'He started hitting me.'

'Damien Lewis. You don't mean he's lost in the woods? How *could* you? I thought we could trust you.'

Donna, who hadn't said a thing up to now, started sobbing quietly, her shoulders heaving up and down. Just then there was a clicking noise as Dad opened the back door.

As soon as he heard the news, he glared at me in a way that meant Big Trouble.

'You'd better take us to where you last saw him,' he said with a frown. 'If we can't find him, I'll have to call the police and get them to launch a search for him.'

The thought of bringing in the police took my breath away. 'Is it *that* serious?' I asked hesitantly.

Dad didn't need to say anything. The dark, worried look on his face showed me just how bad it was.

Mum put her arm round Donna's shoulders and the four of us began retracing my steps. It didn't take us long to reach the spot where Daniel and I had gone our separate ways. A few minutes later, after following Daniel's path, we came across him — climbing trees as usual.

He hardly knew that he was lost and that Mum and Dad had been worried sick about him. When he did find out, he mumbled something like: 'It's Damien's fault. He let me go this way even though he knew it wasn't right.' Trust Daniel to tell another story about me!

Back at home, after Daniel and Donna were in bed, I was given a long lecture on how I needed to be more responsible, especially when it comes to someone Daniel's age. I said, 'Yes, yes' in all the right places — though I'd heard it all before. Then I went to bed, a bit earlier than usual.

Just like normal, I couldn't get to sleep. I lay in bed thinking and worrying for what seemed like hours. I tried everything to get myself to sleep — even counting aliens in space — but it was no good.

'Ah, well,' I mumbled gloomily. 'Up all night *again.*'

Finally, after another three hours at least, I jumped out of bed and tiptoed along the corridor to the bathroom. As I was coming back, I heard Mum and Dad talking in the sitting room downstairs. I didn't have anything else to do so I thought I'd have a sneaky listen.

I was right. It was me they were talking about.

'. . . he just seems to be acting so strange all the time.' It was my mum talking in the kind of whisper you use on stage so that everyone can hear you.

'Maybe a good hiding would solve his problems.

I felt like giving him one after tonight's disaster.' Typical Dad!

'Whatever's bugging him he doesn't seem to want to talk about it.'

'Do you think it would help if I tried to worm it out of him tomorrow after the football match?'

'Might do. If it doesn't, I know this man at church, Harry Hitchin.'

Trust Mum to bring her religion into it.

'He's a full-time leader with a special way of helping people with their problems. Some of the church people joke about him being a great big Care Bear.

'Anyway, he loves kids. Got four of his own, though a few years older than our three. If Damien doesn't open up with you, can I try him?'

'Yeah, I guess so. As a last resort. It's getting a bit desperate.'

Later, as I lay in bed, I began thinking about what my parents had said.

'Maybe I really do need to talk to someone,' I said to the ceiling. 'I can't go on much longer like this. I might end up killing someone.

'One thing's for sure, though. There's no way I'm going to talk about it to some religious nut!'

6

Big Mac

It was the last Saturday of the summer holidays — and the first one of the new soccer season. Dad had bought two tickets for him and me to watch our local City team play their first game of the year. I could hardly wait.

The morning seemed to drag on. I watched a bit of TV, went for a ride on my bike and helped Dad cut the grass. But even then it was only 11.15 on my calculator digital watch.

After what seemed like months, we had a late lunch and soon Dad and I were on the long bus ride to the city centre.

I was wearing a tracksuit with my football shirt in City colours underneath. I used to wear the whole kit under my tracksuit — team shirt, shorts and socks — even when it was a warm day. But I'm a bit old to do that now.

Dad and I both had team scarves, I had a cap and Dad was carrying a City flag to hold up during the game.

We rode in silence, both deep in thought about the forthcoming game. Even though it was only a Second Division team, City stood a good chance of being the league champions this year.

When we changed buses at the centre terminus, we travelled with lots of other City fans and the excitement mounted. Everyone seemed to be talking about our team, discussing the players themselves, the new manager, various tactics for beating the opposition and a host of other things.

My heart was beating with excited anticipation as we joined hundreds of others standing on the terracing. Dad always says that there's not much point in paying extra for seats at a football match — if you're into the game you're on your feet most of the time anyway.

The two teams were out on the pitch for a warm-up when we arrived. Everyone knew it was only a practice so no one took much notice of them. They went back to the changing-room five minutes after we arrived.

Then a table was put in the middle of the pitch and the mayor came on. First he introduced the new manager. There was lots of clapping and cheering and a few people booed. Then the top goal scorer of the previous season was presented with a trophy. *Everyone* seemed to clap and cheer this time.

Soon the pitch was cleared once again. Now, as we waited for the actual game to begin, the excitement grew. It was a bit like the way you feel inside on Christmas eve or on the day before your birthday.

Finally, after what seemed like half an hour but was

really only about five minutes, the ball boys came running on followed by the away team.

Dad was the first on the terracing to shout his support when our team followed them out on to the pitch. He's a quiet man — except when it comes to soccer!

The crowd went wild with excitement when our team ran to the middle of the pitch, lined up and, each putting an arm in the air, turned completely round once.

From then on we were caught up in the chanting and cheering, singing and clapping, as the game progressed. We proudly held up our flag, especially when City's centre forward neatly kicked the ball into the goal. We were going to win!

Seconds before half time a corner was awarded against us when our centre back player accidentally kicked the ball over the touchline, putting the ball out of play. We were a bit shocked when, as a result, the other team scored an equaliser.

At quarter to four I dashed to the refreshment stand to get two hot dogs before the queue got too long. Dad always lets me buy something for us both to eat at half time.

All through the second half we shouted ourselves hoarse trying to urge our team on to victory. Things started looking bad for us when the opposition had a free kick because of an off-side decision. Dad and I thought they'd score, but they missed by a mile.

Even worse was when one of our best players was given a warning by the referee because of a dangerous tackle. Then he was fouled by an opposition player, lost his cool and got into a bit of a fight. His name was written down and we knew he'd be sent off if he had another bookable offence.

Just as our hopes were beginning to fade, our team scored from a penalty kick after a foul by the other team in the 18-yard box. Then the miracle happened. Two seconds before the final whistle, we managed another goal. We had won 3:1! We were really chuffed! I didn't know it was possible to be as excited as this.

As we made our way to the waiting buses, everyone seemed to be wild with excitement. First we started chanting, 'We are the champions, champions of Europe.' Then we sang, 'Going up, going up, going up', over and over again. It was an experience I'll never ever forget.

After a short bus ride to the centre terminus, I was surprised when Dad started walking in the opposite direction to the place where we normally catch the bus home.

'Come on, Damien,' he said in a hoarse whisper, the kind he usually gets after shouting at football matches. 'Let's celebrate!'

Dad's way of celebrating wasn't the same as mine — an evening at the pub or strange foreign food at a posh restaurant. So it was a delightful surprise when, a few minutes later, he led the way into McDonald's.

'This is *my* kind of celebration,' I thought. Then my heart skipped a beat as I remembered overhearing Mum and Dad talking last night. Now I knew the truth. Dad was taking me here so he could force me to tell him what was troubling me.

I was a fly about to be trapped in a spider's web!

A few minutes later I looked at my dad across the plastic-topped table as he popped a French fry into his mouth. Dad has jet-black hair, thinning a bit on top. We make fun of his bald patch but he says it's essential for ventilation or tells us that he's losing his hair to make room for his vast brain.

He's got broad shoulders and big arm muscles — I hope I'm as strong as him one day. His hands are rough and not very nice to look at. When he touches you, it's sometimes a bit like being rubbed with sandpaper!

Dad's always worked with his hands — building, bricklaying, carpentry — you name it, he's done it. Now he's a foreman on a building site but, unlike many other foremen, he still gets involved in the building work itself.

'Hands are the best tools in the world,' he's always saying.

Dad looked up as I began trying to suck thick milkshake through my red, white and yellow plastic straw. It was a bit like drinking ice-cold, chocolate-flavoured concrete.

'What's on your mind, Damien?'

'Oh, nothing really.' I was determined not to make it easy for him.

'Not just now but generally.'

'I don't know what you mean,' I lied in pretend surprise.

'Mum and I are a bit worried about you. You don't seem to be the happy old soul you used to be.'

I suppose I should have opened up with him there

and then. But I couldn't.

It was funny how talking to my parents about sexual abuse seemed so difficult. We're very open and honest with each other about all sorts of other things. Usually when I've got a problem at school or don't feel very happy about something I talk to Mum or Dad about it straightaway.

Sexual abuse seemed sort of different. I can't explain it really. It was as if it was my fault that it had all happened. I imagined my parents would blame me and I'd be punished by not being allowed to go out. And as it was such a horrible thing I'd done, I almost seriously wondered if I'd be kept in every day until I reached the age of 18!

Our teachers at school had discussed sexual abuse. A woman had come specially to talk about saying 'No!' to anyone who wanted to touch your body wrongly. She'd shown us a great video on the subject and said there were people working for the local council who could help.

They also told us about this special group that helps children who've been abused. It's called Childline. The idea is that you phone them up free and they listen to your problem and give you advice. Lots of kids have found it very helpful.

I even wrote their number on a scruffy bit of paper I had in my pocket. Once or twice I'd thought of ringing and telling them about me and Uncle Bill. But I was scared. Really scared. I'm sure it's all right for other kids with the same kind of problem, but I've always preferred to meet someone than talk to them on the phone.

But I couldn't face talking to Dad about it now. I had to change the subject quick — get him thinking that my change of behaviour was for some other reason.

'We all grow up,' I said abruptly.

'Yes, maybe that's it.' Dad put down the cup of coffee in his hand and rubbed the stubble on his chin. I could hear the noisy scratching sound above the din of the other people in the restaurant.

'I remember how, when I was your age, everything was so up and down all the time.' Dad was deep in thought now. My plan to change the subject had worked! 'One day I felt like ending it all and the next I was bursting with excitement. Hmmm, that might account . . . .'

'Oh, you were young once, were you?' I interrupted, hoping to get him even further off the subject of me.

'Now listen to me,' he replied in mock annoyance. 'How many millions of times have you asked me to tell you stories about when I was little? You never doubted *them* before so you must have believed I was young.'

'You could have made them all up,' I taunted, playing for time.

'Coming back to what I was saying' — my plan to change the subject had obviously failed — 'I've noticed how, over the last few months, your body's started to grow up.'

I'd noticed, too. It was embarrassing being so much further ahead than many of my friends at school.

'Around now you'll have all sorts of other changes,'

Dad continued quietly so that no one else could hear. 'I've been thinking it's about time we had a man-to-man chat. In a few weeks' time, maybe at half term, I'm going to take a day off work. We'll go out somewhere — just the two of us — and have a good old talk about things like sex, growing up and all that sort of thing. Right?'

I took an enormous bite of my Big Mac. At the same time I choked back the tears that for some reason had welled up into my eyes.

Dad probably thought I was embarrassed about That Subject.

The truth was I was scared to death. Scared that, when we had our little talk, he would find out about me and Uncle Bill.

My life wouldn't be worth living then.

7

Trapped!

I leaned across as far as I could and tapped Daniel on the shoulder — the one furthest from me. As I hoped, he turned round angrily to the person standing the other side of him.

It happened to be a middle-aged black woman in a straw hat and brightly-coloured dress. I could tell when their eyes met. Hers lit up as she beamed a smile at my little brother. Then she started leaping around in time with the music. It was as if Daniel had encouraged her to do it!

Daniel turned and glared at me through narrowed eyes. 'You wait,' I heard him hiss at me through clenched teeth.

We were at Mum's church. I never thought Dad would come with Mum, let alone bring me and the twins. But Dad was here all right, standing beside me trying to mouth the words of the song we were supposed to be singing — and not making a very good job of it, either.

Dad's always said the only three times worth going to church are to be hatched, matched and despatched (hatched — christening; matched — marriage; despatched — funeral. Get it?).

He was wearing his only suit — the one he gets out for weddings and funerals — and, miracle of miracles, he even had a tie on. The trouble was, he was about the only one dressed up like a dog's dinner. Most of the other men had casual clothes on — trousers and open neck shirts mainly.

Mum's church wasn't like the ones I'd been to for weddings and things. For a start, the people seemed so friendly. I must have shaken hands with at least 20 people before I got to my seat. My hand felt as if it was going to drop off!

Another thing I noticed was that, instead of just a few people scattered around, this place was packed. There were even some standing at the back. I'd guess there were at least 200 grown-ups and loads of children, too.

I always thought church music was slow and old-fashioned until I went to Mum's church. Instead of just an organ or piano they had guitars, drums, flutes and even a synthesiser. The songs were noisy and went with a real swing. In fact, it was much closer to *Top of the Pops* than to *Songs of Praise!*

But the most surprising part was the people themselves. When I first saw them all looking so happy I thought I'd come to a meeting of nut-cases! Then when they started asking us our names and taking an interest in us, I realised that most of them were quite normal.

That's another thing. The few times I'd been to church you had to keep quiet all the time. Even if you whispered, people would turn round and frown at you as if you'd just committed a terrible crime.

In Mum's church before the meeting everyone seems to talk at once. It's like our classroom before the teacher comes — only worse.

Eventually a man at the front stood up, clipped a tiny microphone on his tie and managed to get everyone quiet.

'Good morning, everyone,' he said with a broad smile. 'I'd like to start off by welcoming any visitors we have today. If you're visiting, please stand up.'

Dad and us three kids had to stand, along with quite a few others, while everyone clapped. I was glad when Dad was asked to shout out our four names because then we were allowed to sit down again.

Then the singing started. They sang lots of songs over and over again. Sometimes they'd sing with their eyes closed as if they were pretending they knew every word. At other times they stuck their hands up in the air as if they needed to go to the toilet or they were being held up by a robber.

Then some of the people would start dancing and jumping around the place, looking as happy as a football crowd whose team had just won the cup.

There was one big man on the platform at the front who was leaping around like a fairy elephant. He was very tall — nearly two metres, I'd say — and had steel-rimmed glasses. His greyish hair was swept back but went all over the place whenever he bounced up and down.

He was older than Dad but not as old as my grandparents. I reckoned he was old enough to know better than to dance around like that. He might do himself an injury!

'That's Harry Hitchin, the one I told you might help you-know-who,' I heard Mum tell Dad in her usual stage whisper, pointing from him to me. She could never keep a secret. 'Everyone calls him Harry.'

So that was him! More of a nut-case than I thought.

But worse was to follow. After lots of singing, praying and people going up to the front to say things that I didn't understand, it was notice time. The first announcement was that, because it was the holidays, the children wouldn't be having their own meetings but would be staying in for The Message, whatever that was supposed to be.

The Message turned out to be the longest sermon I'd ever heard. Even more horrible, it was given by Harry — the big man Mum had pointed out to Dad. Just my luck to come this particular week!

As soon as he started, I switched off and began daydreaming. I tried making up names for this church. 'Nuts and Raisins' was one (you know, hand raisings). Just plain 'Nut-house' sounded a bit boring. How about 'Nut Cluster'?

Then I thought of Harry Hitchin. I wondered if he got called 'Hairy Scratch' at school (scratch — itchin').

I was so far gone in my thoughts that I didn't hear a word Harry was saying, only his boring deep voice in a broad local accent as he preached away.

The next thing I knew, all the kids around me had put up their hands. Without thinking, or knowing why, I stuck mine up, too.

'Yes, you, young man.' Harry was pointing in *my* direction! I turned round, expecting to see an older boy sitting behind. No young people there.

Turning back I faced the front. 'Yes, you.' Harry was still pointing at me. 'Come out here and help me.'

With a shock I realised that, unknown to me, I'd just volunteered to do something in front of hundreds of people! 'Well,' I thought, 'if he thinks he's going to make a fool of me, he's got another think coming. *I'm* going to have the last laugh.'

I felt Daniel shoving me at the same moment as I began to get to my feet. Quickly I pushed my way along the row of people and up to the platform at the front. Turning, I almost gasped at the size of the crowd in the room.

'Now, what's your name?' He held a microphone just under my chin.

'Damien,' I replied, more confidently than I thought possible.

'And are you strong?'

'Yeah. Want a fight?' I held my fists up pretending he'd just challenged me to a boxing match. I saw my brother crease up with silent laughter.

'No. But I want to see if you can break this thread.' He held up a cotton reel — the kind my mum uses for her sewing.

'You must be joking,' I said, grabbing a length of the thread and snapping it with one quick pull. It hurt my hand a bit but I'd do anything to make an idiot of this man.

'Now I'm going to try something else. Stand with your arms by your sides,' he said. 'I'll just wrap this thread around you.'

I stood still as he put it round and round my arms and body, then round both my legs. I lost count when he'd wrapped his thread 50 times round me.

'Right, that'll do,' he said after what seemed like ages.

'This is what many people here are like. They're bound by sin, wrapped round by fear and held captive by thoughts of the past. The individual threads themselves are very thin, but when they wrap round and round you they become very, very strong.

'Now, Damien,' he continued. 'See if you can break free.'

I was sure I could ruin Harry's sermon. Tensing my muscles I pushed against the threads with all my might. Nothing happened. I tried moving my arms and legs at the same time — still nothing. By this time my face was hot and I was beginning to panic.

Then I tried wriggling and pushing at the same time. But I was trapped. There seemed no way out.

Finally, in absolute frustration, I stopped struggling. I'd given up to this rotten man.

'Have you tried your hardest?'

I nodded grimly.

'You see, that's what sin, fear and thoughts of the past can do. They hold you. There's no way you can escape on your own.

'But Jesus came to set the captives free. He came to open the prison doors of your life.' He pulled a big pair of scissors out of his jacket pocket and quickly snipped all the threads holding me tight.

'Now you're free, Damien,' he said with a smile.

'You can move your arms and you can walk. How about that?

'Thanks for your help. You can sit down now.'

I stayed rooted to the spot, still with my arms by my sides. This time I was going to make old Hairy Scratch look a proper idiot.

After a few seconds people began to giggle. I heard Daniel's loud-mouthed guffaw, a bit like one of those noisy laughing machines you come across at the seaside. Even Dad and Donna were smiling!

'Come on, aren't you going to move?' Harry put his hand on my shoulder.

I stayed motionless. By now the whole place had erupted into laughter. I'd won!

Quick as a flash Harry (Flash Harry — get it?) changed his tactics. 'Now Damien here is showing us something else about freedom. Some people have been set free by Jesus yet it's as if they're still tied up. They're holding on to the past. They can't let go of those hurtful memories and feelings of hate and anger against people who've wronged them . . . .'

He was back into his sermon now so I quietly crept back to my seat. 'Well done, brother,' whispered Daniel, thumping me on the back in a mock pat. I glared at him but secretly felt pleased with myself at what I'd done.

* * *

That night I lay awake for hours. I kept remembering Harry's prayer at the end of his long, boring sermon. 'Thank you that you've set us free, Lord Jesus,' he'd prayed. 'And if *you* make us free, we really are free.'

Then I started remembering all the nasty things Uncle Bill had done to me. Were those memories of what he'd done holding me like that thread? Was there any way to escape?

Did I really have to become religious to break free — or could I do it by myself?

I fell into a restless sleep, dreaming that I was flying around when I got caught in this giant spider's web. The more I struggled, the more strands of thread seemed to be wrapped round and round me until I was trapped completely.

Then an enormous evil spider started coming towards me. As it got closer I could clearly see its horrible face. Soon it was much bigger than me.

The ugly face looked remarkably like that of Uncle Bill.

8

Harry Hitchin

'Damien. Are you ready yet?' The noisy bellow could be heard all over the city, I reckoned.

'Nearly, Mum.' I was in my bedroom stalling for time.

'Well, hurry up. We'll miss the bus and have to wait another 40 minutes!'

That was just what I wanted to happen, but I didn't let on. Mum was taking me into the city centre to buy some clothes for school. I couldn't think of anything more boring.

At least I didn't have to put up with my pesky brother, Daniel. Grandad had come earlier in the morning and taken him and Donna off for the day.

Typical Mum! It was Monday and the new school term started the next day. I guessed it would be the usual last-minute panic trying to buy clothes for me.

I just hoped they had some decent things in my size. I'd grown so much in the previous few months that my old ones looked ridiculous on me. My trousers only came down to just above my ankles, and when I put my hand up in the air in class, I was sure my jacket sleeve went nearly to my elbow!

Dad explained recently that I was having a growth spurt. 'Maybe we've given you too much fertiliser,' he said jokingly.

Daniel and Donna seemed to be only growing at an ordinary rate so their clothes still fitted them. That's why they were let off the hook and allowed to go to their grandparents' for the day.

Mum and I got to the bus stop with a minute to spare. My scheme to miss the bus hadn't worked. What a bore!

* * *

'A penny for your thoughts,' I heard Mum say above the roaring noise of the bus as it pushed its way back into the traffic from yet another bus stop.

'Oh, er, nothing really. I was just thinking about school.' It was a lie but at least it kept Mum from asking more personal questions.

I glanced at Mum sitting beside me, holding her handbag and folded-up shopping bag on her lap. She'd had her brown hair done in a home perm the previous day. I was glad I hadn't been there. The last time Mum had a perm, Donna said, 'That smell tastes.' I knew what she meant. The strong stink makes your mouth and throat feel funny.

Her hair hadn't settled down yet. It was a mass of curls and looked a bit as if she was wearing a wig.

As usual when she goes out, Mum was wearing lipstick today. I hated her kissing me when she had that stuff on. It always seemed to leave a red mark on your cheek.

Mum is shorter than Dad. In fact, if I carry on growing at this rate, I'll soon be taller than her. Then I can stand up for my rights.

She's a good sort, really, even if I do moan about her. She used to be a bag of nerves, always screaming at us kids and never saying much nice about Dad, either. But since she started going to church and calling herself a Christian she's changed a lot — most of the time, anyway. She still tells me off sometimes, but I guess that's usually for my own good.

It was already busy when we arrived in the city centre. I was surprised how many mums we saw taking little terrors round the shops — and some kids my own age — to get them fitted out for the new school year. Maybe Mum isn't that unusual after all.

Near the station I spotted my friend David from school. He was being dragged along by his mum. His little sister was with them. I shouted hello to him as he passed but he just pretended I didn't exist — unless he's gone deaf over the summer holidays. I suppose he was a bit embarrassed.

We must have gone into every department store in our city that morning. Each time I found something I liked it was either not available in my size or Mum would turn up her nose and say, 'Not on your life,' or tell me to put it back. 'We can't afford *that* amount,' she'd say, as if we were street beggars.

Gradually, though, we started getting the things I needed. Even though they sometimes weren't to my taste and I complained, I was generally pleased with what she'd bought.

Just as I thought my legs would drop off, Mum told

me we'd nearly finished. 'Let's pop into the market for a minute before we get a bite to eat,' she said quickly, looking at her watch.

The market was the usual collection of stalls selling sheets and blankets, fruit and vegetables, baby clothes and dresses. I knew if I stayed with her I'd get bored to death.

'Can I look at the sports stall?' I pleaded hopefully.

'Yes, as long as you stay put until I collect you.'

I didn't need telling a second time. I was there like a shot.

The sports stall consisted mainly of darts and snooker cues — probably because they're so popular on TV. But if you looked hard enough you could find little sections displaying table tennis nets and bats, badminton rackets and cricket balls.

At the side of the stall they had another section where you could buy bits of football gear. That was where I headed for first.

It was interesting looking at the various things for sale. There were shirts and scarves in City's colours — though I had both those myself. There was a decent leather football and a cheap imitation.

Then I noticed little enamel badges showing a football player in City's colours with our team's name in white letters at the top. 'That'd look brill on my new school jacket,' I said to myself.

After I'd walked round the whole stall two or three times looking at everything in detail, I came back to the football section and picked up one of the badges. I rubbed it on the front of my coat to get the fingerprints off. This time it was shining like our sideboard after Mum's used her spray polish.

My decision was made. I reached into my pocket and took out some money. 'This one,' I said to the stallholder, handing him the exact amount. He wrapped my badge in tissue paper and, triumphantly, I put my newly-acquired treasure in my pocket.

I always carried a bit of money from my savings for emergencies like this. Usually it stayed in my pocket for weeks because I was always careful what I spent it on. 'I must remember to put some more money in my trouser pocket tonight,' I thought.

Just then Mum came along. It was easy to tell that she'd been buying things. I didn't bother asking what they were, but I did offer to carry some of the shopping bags for her.

'Come on, slow coach,' she said two minutes later, glancing at her watch yet again. I was rushing to keep up with her. Vaguely I wondered if she'd been practising for the international road-walking championships without telling the rest of the family.

At last we turned into what I thought was an ordinary cafe. Just as we were going through the door I realised with horror that it was part of the building where we'd come to church the previous day. This must be the coffee shop run by the church people that Mum was always telling us about. Why did we have to come here?

It seemed all right though. There were nice tablecloths on all the tables and the chairs looked as if they were handmade. If Dad went there he'd want to have a good look at those chairs, what wood was used and how the joints were made. Mum would be more interested in the vases of flowers on the tables.

And me? I wanted to know what the food was like!

We joined the queue for self-service. There were all kinds of mixed salads on display and the menu on the wall offered mainly strange foreign things like stuffed pitta bread and pasta shells. Give me fish and chips any day!

Mum chose portions of two of the salads and had a piece of cheese and egg pie — the kind with the French name that Dad calls 'Keith and Lorraine'. I settled for a slice of farmhouse pie that had sausage and vegetables in it. I also had some pieces of tomato and lettuce and a baked potato.

When we'd finished I went up to the counter and bought us both some delicious walnut ice-cream in a shiny metal dish. There was a crunchy fan-shaped wafer sticking up in each dish — they really were nice.

All this time Mum kept looking at her watch. That was strange. She didn't usually worry too much about time unless there was something on TV that she specially wanted to watch. Oh, yes, and when Dad was due home from work and would moan a bit if his dinner wasn't ready.

Just as I was hoping that Mum would offer to buy me a drink, I heard a familiar deep voice at the other side of the café. It was Harry Hitchin talking to some of the customers as if he'd known them for years. And he was heading for our table.

That's when it clicked in my mind. Mum's bringing me here was a plot. She'd wanted me to talk to Harry and told him what time to come into the café. I'd been double-crossed.

'Hi, Mary,' Harry said loudly to my mum. 'How *are* you?'

'Fine,' she replied. 'Just doing a bit of last-minute shopping for the new school term with Damien here.'

He looked at me in pretend surprise. 'Well, if it isn't my helper from yesterday . . . . Hello, Damien.'

I nodded in reply.

'Thanks for all your help yesterday. You know something? When you didn't move after I cut you free, it was such a good illustration that I changed my whole message as a result. You might not have realised it but you helped a lot of people break free yesterday.'

I smiled weakly, wishing he'd go away.

'Tell you what,' he continued. 'I'm just about to have a coffee. How about coming up to my office for a drink instead of paying for one down here?'

'What a good idea,' Mum replied for both of us. She was playing the same pretend game that he was. I can always tell when grown-ups are putting on an act.

Harry turned to me. 'Do you drink coffee or would you prefer a cola?'

'Cola'll be OK,' I replied glumly, deliberately forgetting to say 'please'.

Harry bought a can of drink from the counter and then we followed him out of the side door into a hall and up a flight of stairs to the church offices. It was an effort putting one foot in front of the other up the stairs. I remembered from my history books how people about to be executed used to follow the executioner to the gallows. It felt a bit like that now.

His office was about the size of my bedroom — smaller than I'd expected but big enough for him, I guess. There was a desk and chair at one end with lots of Bibles and things in bookcases around the walls. Then there were two or three comfortable chairs nearer the door. When he told us to sit down, I headed for one of them.

As soon as I was given my drink I took a big swig. Seconds later I let out a big burp. Mum said something about being more polite but I just ignored her and took another swig.

Harry tried to get me talking. 'What do you like doing, Damien?' he asked, pushing his steel-rimmed glasses back from the end of his nose.

'Cycling and football,' I replied bluntly, staring at the brown pattern in the carpet. With a bit of imagination it looked like something a dog had left behind.

'Oh, that's interesting. I used to do a lot of cycling when I was younger . . . .'

For the next few minutes he tried his best to get friendly with me while Mum sat in silence, sipping her coffee. He kept asking me 'nice' questions, going on and on about all sorts of things.

Inside I was raging. The only other man who'd ever tried this hard to be friendly with me was Uncle Bill — and look what happened to me as a result!

There was an awkward silence. 'I understand, Damien, that you're — er — going through a bit of a rough patch at the moment.'

'What if I am?' I spat the words out without being able to help myself. It surprised me when Mum didn't tell me off for my outburst.

'I'd like to help you if I can,' he said. 'Lots of folk — young people and adults — need help at different times in their lives. My main job is . . . .'

'I don't need your help!' I interrupted. It was difficult to explain why, but I was trying to be as rude to him as I could.

His gentle reply made me even madder. 'Well, perhaps not now — but when you do need some help or advice, come and have a chat. What you share with me will be in confidence. I promise not to go telling the whole world about your problems!

'I'm here most weekdays between nine and five. Or you can phone me in the evenings at home. Here's my card.'

He handed me a little white card with his name, address and the two phone numbers printed on it. I looked at it for a moment, my heart thumping and my hands sweating with the anger I felt.

'Don't forget, any time you need my help, just let me know. I want to be your friend.'

That last remark made me boil inside. 'You're not my friend.' I spat the words out, screwing up the card into a ball and throwing it across the room. 'You're just like the rest of them.'

My face felt hot as the anger at last bubbled over. *'I never want to see you again, you pig,'* I blurted out, standing up and shouting with all my might.

'I hate you! I hate you!'

9

A lesson learned

I was glad to be on my way to school for the first day of term, though I wouldn't dare admit it to anyone.

The holidays had seemed very long and I'd got a bit bored towards the end. But much worse was the atmosphere in our house since I'd shouted at Harry Hitchin the previous day.

The bus journey home after our shopping trip had been agony. Mum didn't say anything. Not a thing! I think she was too shocked at my outburst. I was shocked, too. I didn't know I had it in me to shout so loud at someone I hardly knew. Especially a grown-up.

Dad, of course, was really angry when he heard what I'd said to Harry. I got a good walloping and then he and Mum spent ages lecturing me on having better manners and all that.

The next morning you could have cut the air with a knife. Everyone was so miserable. Even Daniel and Donna had caught the miseries off the rest of us.

It was good to get out of the house and begin the mile-long walk to school. When it's raining I usually catch the school bus, but normally I prefer the fresh air and exercise. Some of my friends think I'm mad walking when I don't need to, but I enjoy it. Besides, it gives me time to think.

I was looking forward to seeing all my friends again. The only one I'd seen over the summer holidays was David. He'd stayed at our house for a couple of days early in the holidays.

I'd enjoyed it really, even though we'd had quite a few arguments. I was a bit surprised and very upset when, after he'd gone, Mum described him as a self-centred brat. I thought he was great.

As soon as I walked through the school gates I saw in the distance a group of my mates standing in the playground. They were looking my way and seemed to be pointing at me.

Soon I could hear them singing in a noisy, out-of-tune way as if they'd just come out of the pub. I couldn't hear the words, but the tune was that wedding march where you sing:

'Here comes the bride,
Big, fat and wide.'

'Maybe they're singing about weddings because one of them's got a new girlfriend,' I thought.

As I got closer I realised that they were all looking at me and smiling in a nasty kind of way as they sang the same thing over and over again. Suddenly, my mouth dropped open in shock as I caught the words:

'Here comes the queer,
Isn't he a dear?'

And for some strange reason they were singing their song about *me!*

Before I could do anything, they stopped their awful singing and began saying horrible things to me.

'Well, how *are* you, darling?' said a bigger boy as he bent his wrists back like homosexuals are supposed to do.

'It's Damien the dame,' exclaimed another, as if it was the first time *that* joke had been made.

'Where's your lipstick?'

'And your handbag?'

I was speechless. Turning quickly, I walked away from them, hardly believing what I'd just been hearing.

But that wasn't the end of it. All that morning kids kept coming up and saying rude things about me. In science lesson they asked me if I wanted a chemical formula to change sex. In cookery class, some of them suggested I make 'poof' pastry or fairy cakes.

It was all great fun for *them.* They laughed like prize idiots. But it sent *me* into the depths of despair — especially as none of it was true.

What had happened during the summer holidays? Had they all gone mad?

Towards the end of the morning I began to think that my kid brother Daniel had grassed on me about what I'd tried to do to him. But that just didn't seem very likely, especially as he went to a different school.

Then I began to wonder if my friend David had

something to do with it. He was the only person in the world who knew anything about what Uncle Bill had done to me. While he was staying with me, I told him a little bit about it. But surely he didn't think I was a homosexual, did he?

I couldn't concentrate in the maths lesson. The more I thought about it the more I was sure David had told the others that I was 'one of those'.

I remember explaining to David what Uncle Bill had done to me but I guess I'd forgotten to say how horrible I felt about it now. Maybe he thought I was a homosexual and had actually enjoyed being abused!

At lunchtime I confronted David.

'You've grassed on me, haven't you?' I said, putting on my best school-teacher voice.

'What do you mean?' he replied, trying to stop himself from smiling.

'You know.'

'No, I don't. Tell me.'

'About me and my Uncle Bill.'

'Oh, *that.* Who's interested anyway?'

'David, it's not what you think. Uncle Bill might be queer but . . . .' I didn't bother finishing my sentence. David had stopped listening to me and was giggling like a silly little kid.

'Get lost,' I seethed through clenched teeth. 'A fine friend you've turned out to be.' I felt like thumping him but managed to restrain myself just in time.

'See you around, dearie,' he shouted back with a laugh.

As I stood in the playground trying to control the anger that was once again welling up inside me, I remembered how I'd wanted so much to tell someone about Uncle Bill, just to get it off my chest. David had seemed the ideal person at the time, but I guess I'd made a big mistake.

I should have been more careful about who I talked to. If it had been my best friend, Winston, things would have been different. We'd shared all kinds of worries and fears together and I'm sure he never told other people any secrets of mine.

His whole family were a bit like him in that way. I often went around to his house and spent time with his mum and dad and his four brothers. I didn't much like the spicy West Indian food they gave me — except the banana chips — but it was great chatting to them about my worries, hopes and fears.

It taught me a lesson — make sure you pick the right friend when you've got something personal to share. But it was too late now. After this mess, I'd decided never to tell anyone about me and Uncle Bill. Never!

10

Old Murphy

More than anything else, I was dreading the second lesson after lunch on that first day of term.

History was never my favourite subject. I used to joke that it was all old stuff anyway! 'It's in the past now,' I'd say.

But Mr Murphy, our history teacher for the last year, seemed to make it even worse. If you ask me, his lessons were about as stodgy as cold porridge on a winter's day.

We all thought that Old Murphy was a homosexual. He didn't dress like one or talk with a high-pitched voice. But we knew he'd never got married. And whatever period of history he was talking about, he always managed to mention people who, it seemed, had been 'gay'.

It was as if being gay was the most important thing in history. It got really boring after a while.

I once talked to Mum and Dad about Old Murphy.

'One of those radical trendies,' commented Mum, though I didn't have a clue what she meant by that.

'Gay?!' exclaimed Dad. 'Gay used to mean happy

and cheerful. That's one thing most of them aren't. They're usually miserable because deep down inside they know they're wrong. I believe in calling a spade a spade. They're *homosexuals* and that's that!'

Mum nodded. 'God hates homosexual sin — but he loves the sinner.'

Typical Mum-type remark, that. She seems to have black and white answers for everything these days.

* * *

'Good afternoon, class. I trust you've had a good holiday.'

A few of the girls said, 'Yes, thank you.' One boy at the back whispered a loud 'No', but Old Murphy didn't seem to notice.

'This term we're going to look at life in the late 19th and early 20th centuries. That's when your great grandparents were probably quite young.

'But before we start the lesson,' he continued, 'I've heard that the subject of — shall we call it 'sexual identity'? — has been discussed in the playground today.'

It was as if a bombshell had just hit me between the eyes. I knew he was talking about me, and I couldn't believe what I was hearing! Some pig of a so-called friend had spread the rumours about me to Old Murphy, of all people.

'It's not my place to comment on these things,' he said, trying to avoid looking at me, 'except to say that I believe each one of you needs to find his or her own — er — identity.'

He always talked in that kind of pompous way —

a bit like you hear those union leaders on TV trying to be polite about the factory managers they hate so much. I knew what he was trying to say, though. He was actually suggesting that each of us needed to decide whether we were homosexuals or not — at our age!

I could feel the anger in me begin to build up again like a pressure cooker just before it starts making its loud steaming sound. I heard a snapping noise and, looking down, saw that in my anger I'd managed to break my pencil in two!

'Damien, would you be so kind as to pass these books round to everyone in the class?'

I was glad to be given a job. At least it took my mind off my anger. But almost straightaway I wished that someone else had been asked to do it.

'Teacher's pet, now,' sneered one boy as I handed him a history textbook.

'The queer's in Old Murphy's good books,' whispered another.

By the time I'd gone round the whole class and heard the nasty things they were saying about me, I was at bursting point.

'Now life in the closing few years of the last century and the early part of this one was quite a bit different from today,' began Mr Murphy. 'We shall be looking at the kind of houses people lived in, their jobs and lifestyle, food and clothing, the Great War and the kind of entertainment they went to.

'This was the time of the music halls and also plays by that well-known gay playwright, Oscar Wilde . . . .'

'There he goes again,' I sighed to myself. My mind

switched off from what he was saying and I started wondering how I could get rid of Old Murphy. He wasn't very popular at the best of times. I'd do our class some good by finishing him off.

Maybe I could buy a gun and shoot him. Creep up behind him and plunge a carving knife into his back. Or push him through the open window and let him splat on the playground below. I decided against all three of those. I'd only be caught and taken off by the police in handcuffs.

Then I remembered something else they did on telly. I could find Old Murphy's car, get a pair of wire cutters and snip through a thin pipe full of liquid so that the brakes didn't work anymore. Then, when he went down a steep, winding hill, his brakes would fail and the car would crash in a ball of flames.

Just as I was wondering where the nearest steep, winding hill was, I heard Old Murphy say my name loudly.

'Damien! Damien, tell us when it happened.'

'1066.' I said the first date that came into my head. The class erupted into laughter.

'No, the First World War did *not* start in 1066. It was, of course, 1914,' Mr Murphy said after the noise died down. 'The war had a considerable effect on the way people lived . . . .'

I was beginning to drift off into yet another hate-filled daydream when I heard my name again.

'Damien, would you please pop down to the school secretary's office and ask for some coloured chalks? I don't seem to have been supplied with any this term.'

As I walked between the desks towards the door,

the whispered remarks started again.

'What's it like to be in with Old Murphy?'

'It takes a queer to know one.'

'Use the chalk eraser like a powder poof.'

By the time I'd reached the door, my anger had reached exploding point. I was ready to shout with rage or even kill someone. I felt like getting a bomb and blowing up the whole class.

Instead, I slammed the door behind me as hard as I could. For a moment I thought the noise and vibration would bring down half the ceiling — but it didn't.

Then I quickened my pace along the corridor. I walked right past the secretary's office and the headmaster's study. The faster I walked, the more angry I seemed to become.

I raced down the stairs two at a time and headed towards the door into the playground. Once outside, I started running as if I was being chased by American cops. I dashed out of the school gates and down street after street.

I kept looking over my shoulder, expecting my pursuers to be close behind me. But the only signs of life were an old man taking his dog for a walk and a younger woman weeding her garden.

It seemed like an eternity before I dared to slacken my pace, though it was probably only about 10 minutes. Finally, when the coast was clear, I stopped completely.

My face was soaking wet and the shirt under my new jacket was sticking to my body. My chest was heaving up and down as I tried desperately to get enough air into my lungs. My mouth was dry and strangely cold.

I looked around again. There was no one in sight.

My escape had succeeded. But deep down inside my hate for Uncle Bill, Harry Hitchin, David — and now Old Murphy — was still there.

I could escape from others. But was there any way out of these horrible feelings of anger?

11

Jail-break

It seemed like ages before the bus finally came. Every few seconds I glanced around expecting to see a police car or a search party of teachers trying to track me down.

I reached into my pocket and felt the money I'd put in there the night before. It was a relief to know that there hadn't been any other emergencies on that first day back at school.

After climbing aboard, I paid the driver and went quickly upstairs. Usually I try to sit at the front so that I can watch the scene below. This time, even though the bus was nearly empty, I sat at the back, crouched down a bit so I'd be hidden by the seat in front. I wasn't taking any chances.

The bus journey took ages. It was uncomfortable and, with the heating on, almost unbearably warm.

At last we arrived. I made for the nearest shop entrance. From this vantage point I looked around for police cars and any other dangers from my point of view.

When I knew that it was safe I started walking down

the familiar road, weaving in and out among the busy shoppers. There were no other children of my age around — it would be at least half an hour before they got out of school.

I must have stood out like a sore thumb. It felt as though everyone was looking at me. I'd never played truant before and I was beginning to feel very guilty about it.

It was good to reach the building I'd been heading for. I walked in and climbed the stairs. But it must have taken two minutes of hesitating, plucking up courage and then losing it again, before I dared knock on the office door. Even then, my knock was so light that there was no reply.

I tried again, this time knocking a bit harder.

The door opened. I looked up at the face of the man I had so recently met.

'Hello, Damien. It's great to see you. Come in!'

You couldn't mistake that deep, booming voice with the strong local accent. It was only 24 hours since I'd shouted at him angrily. But for some reason that I couldn't really explain, I'd come back to see Harry Hitchin.

'Sit down and make yourself comfortable.'

Without uttering a word, I plonked myself in the same armchair I'd sat in the previous day.

'You look as if you could do with a nice cup of coffee.'

Even though I hated coffee, and it was the last thing in the world I wanted, I nodded dumbly.

Almost as soon as he returned, I wished I'd refused. The coffee in the cup he handed me was dark muddy brown in colour.

It had been made in one of those coffee-makers with a round glass bottle a bit like we use in chemistry at school. I remembered seeing it gurgling away in the corridor yesterday and thinking how revolting the coffee must taste.

I had to smile as I remembered that joke Dad's always telling us about the man who says to the waiter: 'This coffee tastes like mud.' 'Well, sir,' replies the waiter, 'it was fresh ground this morning!'

I heaped three spoonfuls of sugar into my cup hoping to take away the bitter taste. But as soon as I took a sip, I realised that the bitterness was still there. At least it was sweet, wet and warm as well.

We drank without talking for what seemed like an hour, though I expect it was only a couple of minutes. I nearly jumped out of my skin when Harry broke the silence.

'Well, Damien, how can I help you?'

'I — er — I just wanted to say sorry for shouting at you.' That wasn't exactly the reason for coming, but suddenly I had to think of some excuse in case I couldn't bring myself to ask for help.

'That's all right,' he replied. 'You needed to get something out of your system and I happened to be the one sitting in front of you.'

There was another period of awkward silence, this time shorter than before.

'Damien, I believe something happened to you that you find very, very difficult to share with anyone else.'

I stared long and hard at the carpet on the floor. The brown pattern that looked like something left behind by a dog was still there.

'Someone did something to you in the past — and now you blame yourself.'

I nodded and closed my eyes, feeling the searing pain of the memory like a branding-iron on my brain.

'I think what that person did to you was something sexual.'

The words snapped me out of the near-trance I was in. 'Who told you?' I blurted out, rising to my full height and looking sharply at Harry. If he hadn't been so big I would have thumped him.

'No one *told* me, Damien,' he replied gently. 'I've talked to and advised a number of people who've been sexually abused — usually as children — and they often have similar symptoms to yours.

'There was one young mother who almost exploded with rage at me as we talked together about her various problems. I thought she was going to strangle me!

'Eventually the truth came out. Her own father had repeatedly forced her to have sex with him from the age of seven right through into her teens. She'd never talked about it, but just kept it all bottled up inside. She would have ended up with a nervous breakdown if it hadn't all come out.

'You see, even if you try your best to forget these things, they still remain deep down inside. And some day they'll come out one way or another.'

He stopped talking for a second, thinking about what to say next. 'Do you know what happens when you shake a can of fizzy drink for a long time and then open it?'

I nodded enthusiastically. Despite the way I felt,

I couldn't help smiling. I remembered doing it in the school playground once. After shaking the can for about five minutes I went up to a group of my friends and opened it. It sprayed brown fizz everywhere so strongly that I lost half the drink! It was worth it, though. I managed to soak everyone in sight.

Harry continued. 'Yes, the pressure builds up inside to such an extent that it explodes in the end. That's why the first step in the healing process is to talk about these things — before the pressure gets too strong.'

'Now, Damien, how about you beginning at the beginning and telling me the whole sad story?'

A cold chill ran down my spine. It wasn't a nice feeling but at least it helped me get my voice back.

'Why should I?' I snapped. 'I told my friend, David, and now the whole world knows.'

'Look, anything you share won't go outside this room — unless we agree together that it should for some reason.'

We sat in silence for at least another two minutes. 'It — was — my — Uncle Bill.' The words came slowly, hesitantly from my lips. But it felt good in a way to have made a beginning.

'Go on,' said Harry with deep feeling in his voice.

Now that I'd made a start, it was much easier to continue. I told Harry about my birthday treat at the cinema, the visits from Uncle Bill and the day he came into the unlocked bathroom. All the time I was staring at the brown pattern on the carpet.

As I came to the bit about what my uncle did to me in the bath, a lump came to my throat and tears welled up in my eyes. My words were interrupted by sobs that became more and more frequent.

I glanced quickly at Harry. What I saw in that instant made me look again. He was in tears, too!

That made it even worse. The sobs were coming faster and faster like waves on a rough sea. Now I was crying uncontrollably, my shoulders shaking up and down and my face flooded with tears. I could taste the salty flavour as they flowed down into my open mouth.

I felt an arm round my shoulders. Harry had walked across the room, bent down and was now giving me a comforting hug. The stubble of his whiskers rubbed painfully against my face, the steel frame of his glasses was cold on my cheek and, through my own tears, I felt the warmth of the little rivers that ran down *his* face.

For a moment I tensed up, almost expecting to feel his hand begin touching me like Uncle Bill would have done. Nothing like that happened but my instinct was to push him away. He must have sensed that because he said: 'It's alright, Damien. I won't do anything to you.'

I relaxed. For a moment, the only sound in the room was the ticking of a little old alarm clock on Harry's untidy desk. Then I burst into tears again as a fresh wave of memories crowded my already confused mind.

It was five minutes before Harry spoke again. He was sitting back in his chair.

'How do you feel now?' he asked, looking at me intently.

'Much better,' I replied, wiping my eyes with my hanky. 'It's as if a heavy load has been taken off my back.'

'You know, you've made the first step in the healing process by bringing these things out and talking about them. You've opened the can of drink before it could build up too much pressure.

'There's another step,' he continued. 'Tell me, who do you blame for what happened?'

'Uncle Bill, of course.' No sooner had I spoken the words than I realised deep down inside that I really blamed myself. It was a feeling that I kept locked away in my mind.

Harry didn't seem convinced by my answer. He continued to stare at me. It was the kind of look that meant 'Come on, Damien, tell me what you *really* think.'

I let out a deep sigh, resigned to telling the truth. 'Well, I guess it was partly my fault,' I admitted. 'Anyway, Uncle Bill probably wouldn't be in prison if I'd said no to him.'

Harry seemed to think carefully before he spoke again.

'Many people who've been sexually abused blame themselves,' he said. 'Some of them almost feel it was *all* their fault.

'A few feel terrible that in some strange way they actually enjoyed those experiences a little bit.'

My head began spinning and a shudder went down my spine. Somewhere deep down inside that thought had occurred to me from time to time but I'd pushed it down.

'Let me assure you that you were *not* responsible for what happened. Even if you'd been a willing victim — and you would have been very foolish if you had been — it would still have been your uncle's fault. He's an adult; you're a child. It's as simple as that. *Never blame yourself.*'

He let the truth of what he'd just said sink in. I began to feel better than I'd felt for months.

'There's a third step to freedom that's available for you to take,' said Harry. 'Lots of people take the first two steps fairly easily but leave out the third. This step is learning to forgive the person who sexually abused you.'

'Forgive? I'll *never* forgive Uncle Bill. Never!' I said with finality.

'Well, there's no doubt that your uncle did some very, very evil things. He deserved to go to prison.

'Some people make excuses for men like that, saying that their minds were sick at the time. But even if that was true, they don't *have* to do those evil deeds. They have a choice.

'Others talk about them as monsters. Yet God made each one of them. It's only because they *choose* to do wrong that they become horrible.'

I nodded reluctantly. What he said seemed to make sense.

'I suppose you realise that more girls than boys are the target for the sex abuser?'

I nodded again. We'd been taught that at school.

'Many of them are abused by live-in lovers and stepfathers. They find it unbelievably difficult to forgive. Some blame themselves for being too friendly or feel desperately ashamed that they can't cry about it. Others won't let *anyone* touch them or become fat to make themselves less attractive to men. Many, many try to kill themselves.

'One girl I knew about was brought up by her dad from the age of six. Her mum had died in a car crash. Anyway, within a year he was touching her sexually. She didn't like it but was too scared to say anything.

'By the time she was eight, her dad was having full sex with her two or three times a week. She tried to tell people at school, but no one seemed to believe her.

'Now she's 14 and on drugs. And do you know what she does to earn enough money to pay for her drug supply?'

I shook my head.

'She sells her body on the street. She's a prostitute. It's her way of being spiteful to her old man. She's never learned to forgive.

'My wife once helped a teenage girl who had this hatred for all men and boys. She also had the slimmer's disease — anorexia, they call it. By this time she was as skinny as a rake. Everyone was worried that she'd die of starvation before she reached 18.

'Eventually the truth came out. When she was much younger, she would sometimes sleep at her grandparents' house. Quite often, when her grandfather said goodnight and tucked her in bed, he would reach under the bedclothes to feel her body.

'Instead of talking about it to someone, she kept it bottled up until her hatred spread to all men. Her problem with eating that led to anorexia seemed to be a way of trying to stop growing up sexually.

'Then one day she found release from those horrible feelings of hate. She handed over her life to Jesus Christ and learned to forgive her grandfather. Now she's a lovely young Christian wife and mother.

'Of course, it wasn't easy for her having to tell the police the whole awful story about her grandfather. Even worse was standing up in court and being questioned about what exactly happened.

'These days it's a bit easier. Usually they let young people be interviewed outside the court, sometimes on video.'

Harry paused. 'You know something, Damien?' he said suddenly. 'Jesus came to set the prisoners *free.*'

My heart missed a beat.

'You don't mean . . . .'

Harry seemed to read my mind. 'No. I'm not talking about your Uncle Bill coming out of prison. I'm talking about *you.*'

I looked at him in shock.

'You see, your uncle did some terrible things to you. But you've allowed yourself to hate him so much you want to kill him. *You're the prisoner of your own hate.*'

I stared again at the pattern on the carpet.

'I had a man come to see me once. A soldier. Big tough man who had fought in battles all over the world.

'When he was about your age he had to share a room with his uncle. And that uncle used to do the same things to him that your uncle did to you. It went on for months.

'You know what this man said to me?'

I shook my head.

'He said that every time he pulled the trigger — every time he killed a man in the wars he fought — he imagined it was his uncle he was killing.

'He told me that if he ever got hold of that uncle of his, he'd blow his brains out. And he meant it.'

I sucked in my breath, remembering my vicious attack on the bedframe in the shed. I knew just the way he felt.

'But I've got some great news for you. Right now you can be free of those hurts of yours. You can learn to love instead of hate. You can be *free.* Is that what you want?'

I nodded thoughtfully.

He paused. 'May I pray with you?'

It was a prayer a bit like he'd prayed on Sunday — talking to Jesus just like I talk to my friends. It was all about forgiving and being healed inside — that kind of thing. When he'd finished praying, I looked up and our eyes met.

I smiled. For the first time in a year I felt free.

12

The building site

Harry looked at me for a long time before speaking. We had finished our conversation and I was just about ready to leave.

'You're going to have to tell your parents about these things,' he said.

'I know.' It was only a whisper because that was all I could seem to manage.

'I need to tell you another story, Damien.' He hesitated before continuing. 'A girl who had been abused by her father came to see my wife and me. We advised her to talk to her mother about it, which she did. But instead of being sympathetic and understanding, her mother blamed her for what had happened. The parents fell out with each other and, later, the girl had to stand up in court and testify against her own father.

'Her dad ended up in prison and the whole family just seemed to fall apart.

'The point is, Damien, there's no guarantee how your parents are going to react when you talk to them.'

I knew he was right. It was good to be free of those

awful feelings of guilt and hate. If only I could know how Mum and Dad would take the news.

'I'd like to come with you.'

'Thanks,' I replied quietly. At least this way I'd have some support.

'Would you like me to give you a lift home in my car so you can tell them now?'

I shook my head. I wanted to tell Dad first — and he was still at work. Then I had an idea.

'Do you know Orchard Street?'

Harry nodded. It was only a short walk away.

'My dad's helping to build the new office block there. I've been to see him a couple of times so I expect it'll be easy to find him.'

'Right. Let's go, then,' said Harry.

My initial enthusiasm turned to dread as we got nearer to the building site. My feet felt like lead and I wished I could sit down and forget about facing my dad.

At the gate we were given orange helmets to wear. Mine was about three sizes too big for me. But the one on Harry looked ridiculous, perched on his head like a little upturned cereal bowl with a peak to it.

I asked the man on duty at the gate where my dad would be.

'Mr Lewis is probably in the office tidying up after a meeting with the architects and site manager.'

'Thanks,' I said.

The office was really a mobile cabin with clear plastic windows and a few tables and chairs. It's moved from one site to another after each job is finished. Dad's always saying: 'Not many people can say they've got an office that fell off the back of a lorry!'

This was the first time Dad had built a block of offices. Usually he works on houses. I think he enjoyed the change, though he had more paperwork than usual.

When Dad answered our knock on the flimsy door, he almost dropped the two empty cups in his hand.

'Oh — hello — Damien. I didn't expect to see you here.'

He turned to Harry.

And — I believe I met you at my wife's church. Mr — er . . . .'

'Hitchin. But please call me Harry.'

'Yes, Harry. Now what's this son of mine been up to? Nothing naughty, I hope.'

'Can we come in and talk, Dad?' My stomach was fluttering around as if it was full of live butterflies. I wanted to get things over and done with as quickly as possible.

The three of us sat on cheap plastic chairs that had split in places, making them squeaky and uncomfortable.

'Well?' asked Dad, breaking the silence.

'Damien has something to tell you,' replied Harry, looking in my direction. There seemed no way out now.

'Dad,' I started hesitantly, 'you know I haven't been very happy the last year or so.'

'Happy as a wet weekend, if you ask me.'

'Well, it all started because of Uncle Bill.' As I said the last two words, I heard a gasp from my dad's lips.

Looking up I saw that his mouth had dropped open and his face had gone as white as a sheet.

'He — didn't *do* anything to you, did he, Damien?'

'Yes, Dad,' I replied.

'I think you'd better tell him the whole story, Damien,' said Harry.

I did. Beginning with my birthday treat and ending with the episode in the bathroom, I told him as many details as I could. Once I'd started, I found it easier to carry on, especially as this was the second time of telling it.

My story was followed by a long silence. Dad was the one to break it.

'You must have had an awful few months, son. I should have recognised the symptoms,' he said almost in despair. 'We didn't talk much about Uncle Bill after he'd gone to prison, but I guess we should have done.'

He stopped again, weighing up the words he was about to say.

'Damien,' he said in a tone of voice only just above a whisper, 'I think you ought to know that you're not the only one to have been molested by Uncle Bill. Daniel and Donna were as well — even worse than you.'

I gasped in unbelief. 'Yes, it happened over a year ago — probably just before Bill did it to you. Donna was able to tell us almost straightaway so I guess neither of them suffered the months of agony you've been through.

'Daniel said it happened to him in his bedroom one night when Bill was babysitting. He kept shouting downstairs but no-one came to his help. Bill forced him to do some pretty horrible things.'

Waves of guilt swept over me again. I remembered the time. Uncle Bill was upstairs and Daniel kept shouting, 'No!' and 'Help!'. I didn't take much notice because I thought it was just another of my uncle's silly games.

'With Donna, Bill was quite brutal,' Dad continued. 'But I won't go into the details.

'Mum and I were just about to go to the police when we heard that Bill had been arrested. We decided not to tell you anything about the twins or about why Bill was in prison. You seemed to have enough problems of your own. Anyway, we thought you were probably too old for him to be interested in. If only we'd realised . . . .'

Dad's voice tailed off until it was impossible to hear. Then he hesitated for a few seconds.

'I really *do* know how you must've been feeling,' he began again. 'You see, believe it or not, when Bill and I were boys about your age we were both sexually abused by an adult friend of the family.'

I gasped again. I could hardly take in what I was hearing.

'The experience had a serious effect on both of us.' Dad was looking in my direction but he seemed to be staring right through me. 'I had to face the same kind of agonies as you.

'At least I was able to talk about what happened and get it off my chest. But Bill never talked about it. He tried to block it out of his mind.

'As a result, he changed from being a happy, carefree young man to a miserable wretch. We've never been close since.'

Dad hesitated a moment to catch his breath. 'When Bill was arrested and later sent to prison, I guessed why he'd done those horrible things. I reckon it was his warped way of getting his own back on the man who abused us.'

He paused again, his voice choked with emotion and his eyes glistening with tears.

'You know, after Bill was arrested, all the memories of the past flooded back into my mind. I began to blame myself for what happened. I felt like killing the man who did those things. Sometimes I even get the old nightmares of my childhood again.'

Those last few sentences struck a chord in my mind. They were almost word for word my story up to just a few minutes ago.

Instinctively, I walked over to my dad and threw my arms around his neck. It was the first time I'd hugged him in a year. But I couldn't help it.

'It's OK, Dad. I understand,' I said through my own tears.

Then I whispered in his ear as quietly as I could.

'Dad, why don't you have a chat with Harry here,' I told him.

'He'll help you get out of the prison you're in.'

Mr Bill Lewis
Burling Prison
Burling
England

Dear Uncle Bill,

I hope you are well. It must be horrid having bread and water all the time. Dad says prisoners don't like porridge. I think that he was just telling one of his silly jokes.

They used to call me nasty names at school because I told my friend what youd done to me. But now theyve stopped, because I said to them I wasn't gay.

When they let you out, come and see us again. Mum doesn't really mean it when she calls you a scrounger.

I'll beat you at 'Aliens in Space' this time. Only keep your hands to yourself when you come. My body's my own and I belong to Jesus.

My brother, Daniel is still a pain but I guess I like him really. Yesterday he helped me build a tree house. Then we had a meeting in it to decide who can join our gang.

I dont know if you'll ever get this letter. But one thing I'm sure about. I'm not a prisoner anymore.

Love,
Damien